TikTok Takeover 2024

This book discusses the potential for short-form video and social commerce to significantly increase sales through TikTok's e-commerce dominance with Shopify.

Anna P. Moore

All rights reserved. No part of this publication may be reproduced, distributed, or transmitted in any form or by any means, including photocopying, recording, or other electronic or mechanical methods, without the prior written permission of the publisher, except in the case of brief quotations embodied in critical reviews and certain other noncommercial uses permitted by copyright law.

Copyright © Anna P. Moore ,2024.

Table of contents

Chapter one
Chapter Two
Chapter Three
Chapter Four
Chapter Five

Chapter one

Introduction to TikTok E-Commerce

TikTok E-commerce, which uses the popular video-sharing app TikTok as a potent instrument for direct consumer sales, is the fusion of social media interaction with online purchase. TikTok, one of the social media networks with the quickest rate of growth in the world, has evolved from its humble beginnings as to share quick, amusing videos of the platform's features—such as short-form video content, hashtags, live streaming, and interactive elements—to present goods and services in unique and captivating ways that encourage user interaction and streamline transactions. TikTok E-commerce mostly focuses on dynamic, visually attractive material that draws users in as they scroll through their feeds, in contrast to conventional e-commerce sites where customers often browse through static product lists.

TikTok's algorithm, which is renowned for its capacity to customize content and suggest films based on the tastes of specific users, is essential to the success of TikTok E-commerce campaigns. Brands and merchants may efficiently reach their target audience by optimizing their content by using insights on user behavior and preferences. In addition, TikTok's focus on genuineness and user-generated content encourages a community and trust among users, which makes it the perfect platform for businesses to establish a more intimate connection with their clients.

The platform's enormous user base, which crosses demographic and regional boundaries, its immersive and captivating user experience, and its cutting-edge features designed specifically for e-commerce are just a few of the reasons for TikTok E-commerce's success. Furthermore, the addition of shopping features to the TikTok app, such as shoppable advertisements, in-video shopping links, and the "TikTok Shop" feature, has expedited the purchasing process and encouraged users to make impulsive purchases.

Furthermore, it is impossible to overstate the impact that TikTok has on consumer behavior, since viral challenges and trends often cause spikes in demand for certain companies or items. This phenomenon, known as the "TikTok effect," has brought several companies to national attention very immediately, demonstrating the platform's unmatched capacity to increase sales and brand recognition. In conclusion, TikTok E-commerce, which offers a unique fusion of entertainment, creativity, and commerce, signifies a paradigm shift in the way brands and sellers interact with customers online. TikTok E-commerce is positioned to develop into a vital tool for companies wishing to take advantage of social media's ability to propel development and success in the digital era as the platform keeps innovating and evolving.

Why TikTok Will Be Important for Online Shopping in 2024

For companies hoping to prosper in a cutthroat industry, getting ahead of the curve in the ever changing e-commerce scene is essential. One platform in particular stands out as a game-changer in the internet retail space as we approach 2024: TikTok.

TikTok's phenomenal growth and unmatched reach have made it a major player in influencing consumer behavior and buying choices. I examined the reasons for TikTok's emergence as a crucial e-commerce tool in 2024, as well as the many chances it offers companies looking to grow their online presence and optimize their income streams.

First and foremost, it is impossible to ignore TikTok's meteoric ascent to stardom. The site has grown exponentially since its launch, gaining over billions of members globally and securing its place as one of the most significant social media networks of the last ten years. With a user base that is varied in terms of both demographics and geographical areas, TikTok provides companies with unmatched access to a large and engaged audience, making it the perfect platform for worldwide consumer outreach. In addition, TikTok's unique content format—which is comprised of short-form movies that last anywhere from a few seconds to a minute—offers users an engaging and immersive experience that appeals to today's tech-savvy customers. Because TikTok is a user-centric platform, its material is prioritized and shared with users freely, unlike conventional forms of advertising that may seem invasive or obnoxious.

E-commerce companies now have a fantastic chance to highlight their goods and services in a unique way that will grab the attention of their target market and successfully break through the clutter. Furthermore, it is impossible to overestimate TikTok's algorithmic acumen. TikTok's content recommendation engine, which is driven by machine learning and artificial intelligence algorithms, examines user behavior, preferences, and interactions to provide customized material based on the interests of individual users. In other words, companies can use TikTok's algorithm to precisely target their ideal clients, making sure that their material reaches the appropriate people at the right moment to maximize its effect and encourage conversions.

TikTok's e-commerce capabilities have been significantly improved in recent years, adding to its wide reach and captivating content style, solidifying its position as a dominant player in the online retail space. With features like shoppable ads and in-video shopping links, TikTok has made shopping easier for users and turned the platform into a virtual marketplace where users can easily find, browse, and buy products. One such feature is the "TikTok Shop" feature, which allows users to shop directly within the app. In addition, the rise of influencer marketing on TikTok has completely changed how companies interact with customers and increase sales. E-commerce firms may use their reputation and influence to legitimately advocate items from well-known TikTok producers and influencers with significant and devoted followings. This allows them to efficiently reach their fan base and drive traffic to their online shops.

In conclusion, TikTok will be a vital tool for e-commerce in 2024 due to its explosive ascent to fame, unmatched reach, captivating content format, algorithmic skill, and strong e-commerce capabilities. Businesses that integrate TikTok into their e-commerce strategy stand to benefit from greater brand awareness, engagement, and revenue growth in the years to come as the platform continues to develop and change.

An Overview of E-Commerce on TikTok

Overview of TikTok's E-commerce Features: An Introduction to E-CommerceTikTok has quickly developed into a vibrant ecosystem that skillfully combines social interaction with e-commerce prospects, going beyond just being a platform for amusing short-form movies. We'll dive into the many e-commerce capabilities that TikTok provides in this in-depth analysis. These features give companies strong tools to market their goods and services, interact with their audience, and increase sales in creative ways. The capability for companies to designate and optimize their profiles for product sales is one of TikTok's most notable e-commerce capabilities. This involves creating a business account, which grants access to extra advertising and analytics tools designed for e-commerce requirements. Businesses may personalize their shops, show product catalogs, and even highlight special offers or promotions via their profiles.

This allows brands to create a unified brand experience that entices customers to explore and buy straight from the TikTok app.TikTok provides a range of interactive elements, in addition to profile customization, that are intended to improve users' purchasing experiences. Businesses may take advantage of in-video buying buttons, for instance, which let users click on items seen in movies and easily buy them without ever leaving the app. Similar to this, shoppable advertising lets companies advertise their goods via sponsored content that features links that viewers can click to make purchases, thereby converting TikTok into an online store where users can easily purchase things.

On TikTok, live streaming has become a potent e-commerce strategy as well. It allows companies to communicate with their audience in real time and highlight items via interactive Q&A sessions or demos. Businesses may encourage viewers to buy things straight from the broadcast by using tools like shopping stickers and product tagging during live streaming. This creates a feeling of urgency and encourages impulsive purchases. Furthermore, TikTok's algorithmic recommendation engine is a vital component of e-commerce, assisting companies in effectively and precisely reaching their target market. TikTok's algorithm determines each user's interests by examining their behavior, preferences, and interactions. This increases the chance of users engaging with the content and converting. As a result, companies may tailor their content to appeal to the desired clientele, giving their e-commerce campaigns the best possible exposure and effect.

To further expand the potential of the platform, TikTok is always coming up with additional e-commerce services in addition to these fundamental ones. With the launch of the "TikTok Shop" feature, for instance, users now have a dedicated area to find and purchase goods from their preferred brands and creators, opening up new avenues for companies to market their goods and increase sales. To sum up, TikTok's extensive e-commerce capabilities provide companies with unmatched chances to engage with their target market, exhibit their goods, and increase revenue via creative approaches. Businesses may create captivating and immersive purchasing experiences that connect with customers and provide noticeable outcomes by using TikTok's potent algorithm, interactive elements, live streaming, and customized profiles. Businesses that adopt these features stand to benefit from improved brand awareness, engagement, and revenue growth in the ever-changing world of online shopping as TikTok continues to develop and extend its e-commerce capabilities.

Using the Strength of Two Titans: An in-depth examination of Shopify and TikTok

The dynamic pair of Shopify and TikTok is causing quite a stir in the thriving world of e-commerce. This in-depth tutorial explores their synergy and how Shopify enables companies to take advantage of TikTok's enormous reach and engagement potential to grow their e-commerce and endeavors to new heights. Shopify: The Complete E-Commerce Giant Shopify is a full-featured e-commerce platform that gives companies all the resources they need to set up and run their online shops. Here is a sample of what Shopify has to offer:

Effortless Storefront Creation: Create an attractive, intuitive online shop that embodies your brand. With Shopify, you can establish a great shop without knowing a lot of code thanks to its wide selection of configurable themes and easy-to-use editing tools.

Inventory Management: Effectively manage the stock of your products. Keep an eye on stock levels, get notifications when supplies are running low, and make adding new goods to your business easier.

Payment Processing: Customers may easily check out using their chosen payment methods thanks to Shopify's seamless integration with a number of secure payment gateways.

Marketing and Sales Tools: Use the integrated marketing and sales tools to give discount coupons, conduct focused advertising campaigns, and monitor the success of your marketing initiatives.

** Order Fulfillment:** Effectively oversee the order fulfillment procedure. To make sure your clients get their orders on time, print shipping labels, create invoices, and monitor order statuses.

Customer Relationship Management (CRM): To monitor past purchases, manage customer interactions, and customize the shopping experience, Shopify offers basic CRM functions.

TikTok E-Commerce's Ascent: A Path to Millions The massive social networking site TikTok, well-known for its short-form video content, has become a potent e-commerce platform. This is the reason why:

Huge User Base: With billions of active users globally, TikTok offers a huge potential market for your goods.

Highly Engaged Audience: Users of TikTok are renowned for being very engaged, actively engaging with material, keeping up with trends, and learning about new goods.

Short-Form Video Storytelling: This kind of video storytelling makes it possible to communicate compelling stories via inventive and captivating product demos, lessons, and behind-the-scenes looks that draw viewers in and stick with them.

Influencer Marketing Powerhouse: TikTok is a sanctuary for influencers who can market your goods to their devoted fan bases, increasing sales and brand recognition.A dynamic and sociable buying experience is fostered by the live stream shopping features, which include unique deals, interactive Q&A sessions, and real-time product demos.

The Power Couple: Shopify and TikTok

Shopify and TikTok have forged a strong collaboration that enables companies to easily connect their online storefronts with the dynamic TikTok e-commerce platform. This equates to success as follows:

Effortless Product Syncing: You can easily sync your product catalog from your Shopify shop to your TikTok profile using the Shopify app for TikTok. This guarantees that product information is constantly current and does away with the need for human data entry.

Shoppable Video Ads: Produce eye-catching video advertisements that highlight your merchandise, then seamlessly include them into your TikTok content plan. When viewers click the advertisement, they will be sent directly to your Shopify shop, where they may easily finish their purchase.

Analytics and Conversion Tracking: Monitor the success of your TikTok marketing campaigns. Shopify gives you useful information on how sales from your TikTok presence affect your online business.

Streamlined Order Management: Control every order from one central location, whether it comes from your Shopify shop or your TikTok profile. Order fulfillment and inventory control are made simpler as a result.

Advanced Strategies for Success: Going Beyond the Basics Although the Shopify app offers a strong starting point, the following extra tactics will help you succeed more on TikTok:

material is King : Provide unique, interesting TikTok material that appeals to your target demographic. Go beyond standard product presentations to engage listeners with anecdotes, beneficial demonstrations, and humorous or timely challenges.

Accept User-Generated Content (UGC): Motivate clients to provide media that highlights your offerings. UGC promotes genuineness, increases trust, and highlights the practical benefits that your products provide.

Influencer Marketing Magic: Collaborate with relevant TikTok influencers that share the same values and goals as your target market and company.

Take advantage of their popularity and authority to market your goods in a sincere and approachable manner.

Live Stream Like a Pro: In order to increase sales and audience engagement, host engaging live broadcasts with influencer partnerships, product demos, special offers, and competitions.

Final Thought: A Harmony of Achievement

Shopify and TikTok's perfect partnership provides a potent symphony for the success of e-commerce. By using Shopify's extensive capabilities, you can easily manage your online business.

Chapter Two

Establishing an E-Commerce Store on TikTok: Establishing a Business Account on TikTok

Building a strong social media presence has become crucial for companies looking to successfully connect with and interact with their target audience in the constantly changing world of digital commerce. TikTok has become a dominant force in social media marketing because of its phenomenal growth and unmatched reach. It provides companies with exceptional chances to present their goods and services to a large and interested audience. In this in-depth investigation, I will go into detail about how to create a business account on TikTok, offering step-by-step instructions on how to use this potent platform to open an online shop and increase sales.

Making a business account on the TikTok platform is the first step towards establishing your online shop. Business accounts come with extra features and capabilities, especially those made to promote marketing campaigns and e-commerce, in contrast to personal accounts, which are mainly meant for individual users to share personal material with friends and followers.

The first step in creating a business account on TikTok is to download and install the app on your smartphone from the App Store or Google Play Store. To access your profile settings, go to the bottom right corner of the app's home screen and press the "Me" button. The settings menu can then be accessed by tapping the three-dot (ellipsis) menu icon in the upper right corner of the screen.Scroll down to the "Manage my account" option in the settings menu, hit it, and choose "Switch to Pro Account" from the list of possibilities. Two kinds of business accounts are available on TikTok: "Creator" accounts, intended for users or influencers who post content on the site, and "Business" accounts, intended for companies and organizations trying to advertise goods or services.Once you've chosen the "Business" account option, you'll be asked to pick the category that most accurately fits your company.
There are many other categories available on TikTok, such as technology, cuisine, fashion, beauty, and more. By choosing a category that corresponds

with the sector or specialty of your company, TikTok will be better able to identify your target market and provide them with content recommendations. After selecting a category, you'll need to provide further details about your company, such as your name, website address, and contact details. Users may connect with you outside of the platform and learn more about your company by seeing this information on your TikTok profile. After reading the privacy statement and terms of service, establish your company account by clicking the "Confirm" button.

You've created a business account on TikTok, which is a great first step towards opening an online store and connecting with millions of potential customers on one of the most widely used social media platforms worldwide.

The first step in establishing an e-commerce shop and taking advantage of TikTok's enormous potential for increasing sales and expanding your company is to create a business account. You can create a strong online presence on TikTok and use its robust features and tools to effectively connect with your target audience, highlight your products, and drive conversions by following the above-described step-by-step instructions.

Configuring Your TikTok E-Commerce Store: Configuring and Personalizing Your Online Store

In the fast-paced world of online shopping, having a strong social media presence has become essential for companies trying to engage with their target market and increase revenue. With its enormous user base and captivating content style, TikTok has become a dominant force in the field of social media marketing, providing companies with exceptional chances to highlight their goods and interact with clients in novel ways. We'll go over how to set up and customize your e-commerce shop on TikTok in this in-depth tutorial, complete with best practices and step-by-step instructions to help you launch your store effectively and get significant results.

1. **Using the E-Commerce Features on TikTok**: It's crucial to confirm that you have access to TikTok's e-commerce tools before you can create your online shop. Check to see whether your account qualifies for e-commerce features including

shoppable advertisements, in-video shopping links, and the TikTok Shop feature as of 2024. TikTok's e-commerce capabilities may differ based on your area and kind of company.

2. **Enabling E-commerce Capabilities: Once you've validated that your account is suitable for e-commerce capabilities, you'll need to activate these services inside the TikTok app. Locate the e-commerce or business feature enablement option by navigating to your account settings. To enable e-commerce capabilities for your account, just follow the instructions. This will provide you access to a variety of tools and services designed to help you with your TikTok e-commerce endeavors.

3. **Building Your E-Commerce Business: Now that you have access to e-commerce tools, you can start configuring your TikTok e-commerce business. To begin, go to your profile settings and search for e-commerce or storefront customization choices. It's possible that TikTok may provide templates or wizards to help you build your online shop and easily add product listings, banners, and promotional material to your storefront.

4. **Adding Product Listings**: Product listings, which let you display your items right on your profile, are an essential part of any TikTok e-commerce business. Upload pictures or videos of your items, together with their pricing, descriptions, and any other pertinent information, to create product listings. To make your items more appealing to prospective buyers, think about highlighting their features and advantages using eye-catching imagery and persuasive writing.

5. **Customizing Your Storefront**: Make your online storefront unique to your business so that customers have a seamless purchasing experience. This might include altering the layout, colors, and typefaces of your profile banner to better suit your brand's style and improve the appearance of your shop. To attract customers' attention and encourage interaction, think about prominently displaying particular items or promotions on your storefront.

6. **Optimizing for Mobile**: Remember that TikTok is a mobile-first platform, so you should make sure your online store is mobile-friendly. Make sure your mobile shop has clear calls-to-action and user-friendly navigation menus, and that it is

both aesthetically pleasing and simple to use. To guarantee compatibility and responsiveness and to provide customers with a flawless buying experience on any platform, test your storefront on a range of mobile devices.

7. **Promoting Your business**: In order to draw customers and increase sales, you need to market your e-commerce business once it has been set up and personalized.

Make use of TikTok's advertising features, such as shoppable advertisements and sponsored posts, to expand your audience and increase traffic to your business. Create interesting content as well, showcasing your goods in unique and captivating ways to entice customers to browse your shop and buy.

Therefore, it takes careful preparation, close attention to detail, and a deliberate approach to branding and advertising to set up and customize your e-commerce business on TikTok. You may build an engaging shop that draws customers, increases revenue, and aids in the accomplishment of your e-commerce objectives by following the above-mentioned procedures and making proper use of TikTok's e-commerce tools. Your TikTok e-commerce site has the ability to develop and succeed in the ever-changing world of online retail, becoming a valuable asset for your company with the correct plan and execution.

Chapter Three

Developing Skillfully at the Scroll: Creating Powerful TikTok Advertising for Online Retail

Successful e-commerce requires creating compelling advertisements in the fast-paced world of TikTok, where consumers' attention spans are short and competition is intense. With the knowledge and skills in this chapter, you will be able to effectively traverse the variety of TikTok ad formats and customize your message to effectively reach and convert your target audience.

Explosing the TikTok Advertising Fleet
TikTok provides an array of dynamic ad types, each tailored to meet distinct marketing goals. The first step in creating effective advertising campaigns is comprehending these options:

In-Feed Ads: These imitate genuine material by blending in with user feeds. These might be brief (60 seconds or less) video advertisements or picture advertisements with an obvious call to action. Because of their great adaptability, in-feed advertisements are ideal for promoting your brand, showcasing products, and increasing traffic to your online shop.

Spark Ads: These encourage user-generated content (UGC) that highlights your business or product by using the power of organic content. Spark Ads increase prospective consumers' confidence and credibility by showcasing real testimonials and reviews.

Top View Ads: For the first few seconds after an app user opens it, these premium placements fill the screen. They are perfect for introducing new items or making a big brand impression since they provide tremendous impact and brand awareness.

Branded Hashtag Challenges: In this interactive style, viewers are encouraged to utilize a predetermined hashtag to make their own films. Branded hashtag challenges build community around your product, increase brand exposure, and dramatically increase user engagement.

Collection Ads: Immersive advertisements that feature many goods in one piece. Viewers may easily browse to your online shop to make purchases by swiping through product photos or videos, exploring information, and making purchases. Product lines or well chosen collections are ideal for promotion via collection advertising.

Selecting the appropriate weapon for the battle

When you have a variety of ad formats at your disposal, the best format to choose depends on your unique marketing objectives.

Here is a summary to help you make a decision:

Brand Awareness and Discovery:
Attention-grabbing advertisements like In-feed commercials, Top View commercials, and Branded Hashtag Challenges are excellent ways to get your brand in front of more people.

Engagement and Community Building:
Create a community around your goods, stimulate user involvement, and create brand loyalty using Spark Ads and Branded Hashtag Challenges.

Increasing Traffic and Conversions:

Collection advertisements and in-feed ads with obvious calls to action simplify the user experience by facilitating viewers' discovery, exploration, and purchase of your items.

Maximizing the Impact of Your Ad Creative
Creating effective ad creative is just as important as choosing the right format.

Here are a few essential components for success:
Hang them in the First Frame: Since viewers' attention spans are limited, capture their interest in the first few seconds using eye-catching imagery, a relevant narrative, or a funny element.
Feature Your Products in Action: Provide examples of how your products improve lives, solve problems, or add value. To establish credibility and trust, take advantage of influencer endorsements, user-generated material, and high-quality images.
Short and Sweet: Appreciate TikTok's quick-paced environment. Within the constraints of the timetable that your selected ad format allows, strive for succinct and powerful messaging.

Acknowledge the Power of Music and Sound Effects: These elements can greatly increase the emotional impact of your advertisement. Select components that work well with your brand and appeal to your intended market.

Include a Clear Call to Action: Specify for viewers what you want them to do after viewing your advertisement. Make the intended action obvious and simple to do, whether it's installing your app, visiting your website, or making a purchase.

You can unleash the enormous potential of this platform for your e-commerce business by comprehending the wide range of TikTok ad types, matching your selection with your marketing objectives, and creating an effective ad creative. Recall that effective TikTok advertising depends on adhering to the platform's core values of creativity, authenticity, and engaging content (CAC).

Building Your Online Business: Creating Winning TikTok Advertising Campaigns
Overcoming the constantly changing TikTok e-commerce market demands a calculated strategy. This chapter explores the core of creating and

implementing successful TikTok advertising campaigns, enabling you to turn your brand's message into an engaging force that increases engagement and sales.

Building the Base: Audience Targeting and Campaign Objectives

Creating a clear blueprint is essential before creating any ads. This is what you should firmly believe:

Determining Your Campaign Goals: Do you want to increase direct sales, increase website traffic, or raise brand awareness? Identifying your core aim determines the direction of your overall marketing plan.

Knowing Your Audience: Understanding your target consumer is crucial. Conduct detailed audience research to uncover demographics, interests, and online activity patterns. Make use of TikTok's robust targeting capabilities to make sure the most responsive viewers see your advertising.

The War Room: Configuring Your Manager for TikTok Ads

Your command center for the operation is TikTok Ads Manager. The following is a summary of the essential steps:

Opening a TikTok Ads Manager Account:
With this free account, you can create campaigns, set budgets, and monitor performance.
Creating Your Campaign:
Specify the goal of your campaign, the limits of your money, and the length of your campaign.
Crafting Ad Groups:
Identify target audience segments or marketing goals. This makes optimization and control more precise.
Choosing Your Ad type: As discussed in the previous chapter, choose the ad type that most closely corresponds with the objectives of your campaign.

Building Your Ad Creative Arsenal: Crafting Compelling Content
Now that the technicalities are taken care of, let your imagination run wild:
Creating Captivating Ad Concepts: Keep in mind that there are a ton of short-form videos out there vying for viewers' attention. Create ideas that are captivating to the eye, emotionally poignant, or lighthearted.
Visual Storytelling: TikTok is a story-driven platform. Present your items in use, include client

endorsements, or make use of influencer collaborations to create relevant and genuine stories.

Mobile Viewing Optimization: Remember that the majority of TikTok users access content via smartphones. Make sure the creative for your advertisement is scaled correctly and provides a smooth viewing experience.

Including Strong Calls to Action: Don't leave your audience in suspense! Indicate to them exactly what you want them to do—visit your website, get more information about a product, or make a purchase—after they view your advertisement.

Allocation of Budget and Bidding Strategies:

The secret to a successful campaign is budget allocation optimization. Here are some things to think about:

Bidding Strategies: You can decide how much you're willing to pay for particular actions, such as clicks or conversions, using the different bidding options that TikTok offers.

Distribution of Budget: Spread your funds wisely across various ad groups and formats according to their effectiveness and possible return on investment (ROI).

The Last Frontier: Starting and Tracking Your Ad
Now that you've carefully designed your campaign, it's time to present it to the TikTok audience:

Campaign Launch: Check your settings, make sure everything is in working order, and eagerly begin your campaign.

Performance Tracking: Utilize TikTok Ads Manager's full analytics package to monitor important metrics, including impressions, clicks, conversions, and cost-per-acquisition (CPA).

Campaign Optimization: Make constant improvements to your campaign based on performance data. For best results, optimize your budget allocation, tweak targeting settings, and do A/B tests on various ad creatives.

A combination of data-driven optimization, creative execution, and strategic planning is needed to create effective TikTok advertising campaigns. Your e-commerce company may become a dominant force on TikTok by adhering to these guidelines and the platform's basic principles of engagement and entertainment. Recall that the keys to success are knowing your audience, creating engaging content, and regularly modifying your plan in light of performance data. So, unleash your imagination, embrace innovation, and see your brand connect with the passionate TikTok community.

Hitting the Bullseye: Targeting the Right Audience for Your Products with TikTok Ads

In the changing world of TikTok e-commerce, making appealing advertising is just half the battle. Making sure your message reaches prospective clients who are really interested in what you have to offer is where the real power is found.

This subchapter gives you the tools to identify your targeted audience and make the most of it by using TikTok's robust targeting capabilities.

Breaking Down the Myths Around Audience Targeting

Reaching the correct audience is important to the success of any marketing campaign. Here's how TikTok permits you to reach laser-like accuracy in targeting:

Demographic Targeting:

Drill down to particular demographics like age, gender, location, economic level, and even device kind. This enables you to modify your message so that it appeals to certain demographic groups.

Interest Targeting: Target people according to their interests to go beyond demographics. Use the vast data pool that TikTok offers to target people who have shown interest in certain pastimes, pursuits, or product categories. If you offer sportswear, for instance, focus on people who have interacted with exercise material.

Behavior Targeting: Utilizing this sophisticated targeting feature, you may connect with people who have used the platform in a certain way. Users who have already engaged with rival material, viewed videos about comparable items, or clicked on relevant hashtags should be your target audience.

Lookalike Audiences: With the help of this effective tool, you may reach a wider audience by focusing on people who resemble your current clientele. Create a "lookalike audience" by using the customer data you already have on file to reach more prospects who are likely to become customers.

Understanding TikTok User Behavior

Understanding user behavior on TikTok is essential for efficient audience targeting, even beyond the technical features:

Consumption Habits: Users of TikTok interact with material in a proactive manner. Go for viewers that regularly interact with content producers in your niche, watch videos about your product category, or take part in challenges that are pertinent to them.

Popular Sounds and Hashtags: Take advantage of popular sounds and hashtags in your field. By focusing on people who participate in these trends, you can capitalize on their popularity and reach a larger audience that is more open to your message.

Influencer Marketing Integration: Collaborating with relevant influencers who share a common interest with your target market can be an effective means of reaching that audience. Use influencer marketing to connect with a pre-engaged audience that values the recommendations of the influencer.

Developing a Targeting Strategy Across Multiple Dimensions: Targeting successfully requires a multifaceted strategy, which includes:

Layering Targeting Options: Create a focused net that catches your ideal consumer by combining demographics, interests, behaviors, and lookalike audiences.

Using A/B Testing: Experiment with various targeting configurations to see which ones your audience responds to the best. You can maximize your return on investment (ROI) and continually improve your plan with this data-driven method.

The Effectiveness of Retargeting

Never undervalue the effectiveness of retargeting. You may connect with people on TikTok who have already engaged with your brand—perhaps via a prior visit to your website or advertisement—by reaching out to them. Campaigns for retargeting users may be quite successful in reminding them of your brand and encouraging them to convert.

Accurate Targeting for Successful E-Commerce

Your TikTok advertisements may become laser-focused weapons by learning the art of audience targeting. This will allow you to reach prospective consumers who are ready to interact with your brand and become devoted customers. Recall that effective targeting requires a combination of user behavior studies, data analysis, and ongoing optimization. Take advantage of

TikTok's targeting choices to help your e-commerce firm grow and expand.

The Alchemy of Conversion: Crafting High-Converting Ad Creatives for TikTok E-commerce

In the fast-paced world of TikTok e-commerce, compelling ad creatives are the magic elixir that turns viewers into paying consumers.

This subchapter looks into the secrets of producing high-converting ad text, ensuring your message connects deeply, awakens a demand for your items, and eventually generates sales.

The Art of Storytelling in a Short-Form Format
Attention spans are brief on TikTok. Use narrative to captivate audiences in a matter of seconds. Here's how to quickly create an engaging story in a short amount of time:

Capture Them in the First Frame: The first few seconds matter. To draw in visitors and pique their interest, use eye-catching imagery, a realistic issue situation, or a hint of comedy.

Showcase items Solving Problems:
Showcase items' worth rather than merely showcasing them. Emphasize how your products improve lives, address difficulties that arise every day, or infuse routines with a little enchantment.

Insist on an Emotional Bond:
People make purchases based on their feelings. Showcase happy consumers utilizing your goods, touching testimonies, or hilarious situations where your product plays a crucial role in eliciting positive feelings like joy, enthusiasm, or a sense of belonging.

Embrace genuineness:
Gen Z, the majority of TikTok's user base, is drawn to genuineness. Steer clear of planned, highly polished material. Use influencer relationships that seem authentic and relevant, or use user-generated content (UGC) that shows actual people using your items.

The Influence of TikTok Visual Storytelling

Any good TikTok advertisement relies heavily on its visuals. Here's how to use them to your fullest advantage:

Exceptional Video Production: Aim for crisp, captivating images that best represent your items, even when high-end filming isn't necessary.

Editing at a Fast Pace: Ensure that viewers are kept interested by using fast cuts, dynamic edits, and transitions that preserve a feeling of excitement and urgency.

Live Product Demonstrations: Don't only display still pictures. Present your items in use, emphasizing their salient characteristics and advantages. To highlight the elegance and practicality of your products, use close-ups, slow motion, and unique camera angles.

Incorporate text overlays: Text overlays may highlight important aspects and improve comprehension. Make use of attention-grabbing fonts that go well with your overall advertising style and succinct, clear messaging.

The Urge to Act: Your Ultimate Conversion Booster

Conversion rates may only be increased with an effective call to action (CTA).

How to create one that works is as follows:
Details are Crucial: Specify for viewers what you want them to do after your advertisement. Would you like them to click through to your website, download an app, or buy something? Be precise and straightforward.

Sense of Urgency: Use CTAs that promote quick action to instill a sense of urgency. Make use of expressions such as "Don't Miss Out," "Shop Now," and "Limited Time Offer."* **Simple Implementation:** Make it simple for visitors to click on your call to action. Add easy-to-find download buttons for your program, obvious website URLs, or straightforward directions like "Swipe Up to Learn More."

Creative Optimization and A/B Testing Constant tuning is the secret to creating ad creative that converts well. Here's how to keep on top of things:
A/B Test Different Variations: Experiment with various ad wording, images, call-to-actions, and editing techniques to see which ones your audience responds to the best. Use TikTok's A/B testing

features to collect information and improve your creative approach.

Remain Up to Date on Trends: TikTok is a trend-driven platform. To grab attention and ride the virality wave, keep an eye on what's popular and incorporate trending elements into your ad creatives, such as music, challenges, or dance moves.

Influencer Marketing's Power

Partnering with relevant TikTok influencers might be a game-changer for your ad creatives. This is the reason why:

 Leveraging Established Trust: Influencers have developed trust and credibility with their audience. By engaging with the proper influencer, you can tap into their current popularity and profit from their support of your items.

Authentic Product Integration: The greatest influencer collaborations seem natural and genuine. Encourage influencers to exhibit your items in a manner that resonates with their style and content, producing a smooth and genuine integration.

** The Recipe for High-Converting Ads**

Creating visually stunning ads with a strong call to action and engaging narrative is a skill for creating high-converting TikTok ad creatives. By embracing the power of short-form tales, focusing on visual appeal, and consistently tweaking your strategy, you can turn your TikTok commercials into magnets that draw viewers and convert them into devoted customers.

Demystifying the Data: Monitoring and Examining the Results of Your TikTok Advertising to Ensure E-Commerce Success

Creating effective advertising campaigns is just the first step in the dynamic world of TikTok e-commerce. Careful monitoring and analysis of your ad performance is essential to maximizing your return on investment (ROI) and realizing your full potential. This chapter gives you the skills you need to successfully navigate the TikTok Ads Manager analytics environment and turn data into insights that can advance your e-commerce company.

Discovering TikTok Ads Manager Analytics' Power: With its extensive set of analytics tools, TikTok Ads Manager gives you a clear picture of the effectiveness of your campaigns. What you can learn from this data gold mine is as follows: Track important data like impressions, clicks, conversions, cost per click (CPC), cost per acquisition (CPA), and click-through rate (CTR) to ensure your campaign is performing as intended. These data provide you with a clear sense of the reach, degree of engagement, and overall efficacy of your advertisement in generating sales.

Audience Insights: Examine performance statistics broken down by geography, gender, age, and device type to go further. This enables you to determine which audience groups are most receptive to your message and adjust your targeting approach appropriately.

Content Performance Analysis: Examine the effectiveness of each unique ad creative in your campaign. Determine which advertisements result in the most clicks, purchases, and conversions. Use this data to develop your creative approach and prioritize the message that connects most with your target demographic.

Placement Breakdown: Examine the performance of your advertising on TikTok across various placements, such as the "For You" feed or in-feed placements. You can maximize your return on investment and optimize your budget allocation by knowing which placements provide the greatest outcomes.

Comprehending Crucial Metrics for E-Commerce Achievement

Even if there are many indicators available, success in e-commerce depends on concentrating on the following:

Conversions: This indicator shows how well your advertisements promote revenues; it's often assessed via website purchases or app downloads. Make campaign optimization a top priority in order to increase conversions.

Cost per Acquisition (CPA): This indicator shows you how much it usually costs you to get a conversion from your advertising campaign. In order to be sure that your advertising is yielding a good return, concentrate on reducing your CPA.

Return on Ad Spend (ROAS): This measure shows how much money you make for each dollar you spend on advertising. A high ROAS indicates that the sales you are generating from your advertising are lucrative.

Using Data to Drive Ongoing Improvement Refining your approach with data is where analytics really shine.
 Here's how to put your knowledge into practice:

A/B Testing Optimization: Make use of the data to determine which budget allocations, target specifications, or ad creatives work best. Iterate your strategy and do ongoing A/B tests to get the best possible outcomes.

Audience Refinement: Concentrate your targeting approach on the interests and demographics that result in the best conversion rates based on your data. Get rid of failing audience segments to make sure the most responsive viewers get your funding.

Content Iteration: Based on data analysis, you may determine which creative components and ad formats work best for your target demographic. Use this data to select content aspects that increase engagement and conversions and to improve your content strategy.

Expert Analytics Methods for Influential Users: TikTok Ads Manager provides capabilities for comprehensive analytics.

Funnel Analysis: With this tool, you can see where prospective buyers stall out throughout the conversion process by visualizing the user journey. By identifying these drop-off spots, you may solve bottlenecks and enhance your landing pages or user experience for better conversions.*

Attribution Modelling: This cutting-edge function aids in your comprehension of the many touchpoints that influence a conversion. You may ascertain if your advertisements are the only factor influencing conversions or whether they complement other marketing initiatives by examining attribution data.

Using Data to Its Full Potential

Adopting TikTok Ads Manager analytics gives you access to a wealth of information that helps you maximize the effectiveness of your e-commerce advertising campaigns. Convert unprocessed data into useful insights, iteratively improve your approach, and see how your TikTok advertising efforts develop into effective catalysts for boosting revenue and attracting new clients. Recall that data is your friend; use it to your advantage to remain ahead of the curve, make wise choices, and guarantee that your e-commerce company succeeds on TikTok.

Chapter Four

The Order Fulfillment Tango: Successful TikTok E-commerce Through Efficient Order Processing

Effective order fulfillment is the deft job that keeps your clients satisfied and your company prospering. With the information in this chapter, you will be able to optimize your order processing processes, guaranteeing prompt delivery and a satisfying client experience that will encourage repeat business.

Click to Delivery: The Process of Order Fulfillment Optimization requires an understanding of the order fulfillment process. The following is a summary of the essential steps:
Notification and Order Receipt: You are notified when a consumer purchases anything from your integrated online shop or TikTok Shop. The order processing procedure is triggered by this.

Payment processing and order verification: Check the order details, such as the delivery address, product selection, and client information. Make sure that the money is processed securely, and verify the transaction.

Selection and Inventory Check: Verify that the goods you purchased are in stock. To identify and choose products quickly, make use of a well-organized storage system or a powerful inventory management system.

Preparing for Shipping and Packing: Make sure the goods are packaged neatly and safely to ensure that they are safeguarded throughout transportation. Make mailing labels, figure out how much shipping will cost, and choose a dependable shipping company based on both price and timeliness.

Order Tracking and Dispatch Details: Send the order out via the selected carrier, and provide your client access to tracking details as soon as possible. This enables users to track the status of their product and predict delivery.

Streamlining the Workflow for Order Processing
Reducing processing times and satisfying your consumers depend on efficiency. Here are some methods to improve the efficiency of your business:

Invest in software for inventory management: Go beyond spreadsheets. Order picking guidelines, stock level monitoring, and even integration with shipping carriers are all automated by inventory management software, which also streamlines workflow.

Create a System for Picking and Packing: Set aside certain spaces for packing and selection. Reduce the amount of time you spend looking for items by putting in place a clear method for organizing your inventory.

Selection in Bulk: If you have a lot of orders, you may want to think about batch picking. Select products at the same time from many orders to save time and reduce traffic in the warehouse.

Typical Package Contents: To expedite the packing process, spend money on premium, pre-sized packaging supplies. Order processing may also be sped up using pre-printed packing slips.

Partnership is Crucial: Integrate your shipping carrier accounts, inventory management system, and online retail platform. This may even do away with the need for human data input by automating the creation of labels and the transmission of order data.

Creating an Efficient Culture

It is essential to cultivate an efficient culture in addition to software and infrastructure. Here are some pointers:

Clear Communication: Make sure the fulfillment and sales teams are communicating clearly with one another. Accurate order information and timely order placement notifications are essential for effective processing.

Employee Training: Educate your personnel on inventory control, correct packaging methods, and order processing protocols. A proficient team is a productive team.

Observation of Performance: Keep an eye on important order processing data, such as picking accuracy and average processing time. Locate bottlenecks and take remedial action to keep your productivity rising.

The Efficiency Recap: Effective order processing is a continuous performance that keeps your company in step with the needs of TikTok e-commerce while also satisfying your clients. You can make your order fulfillment process a well-practiced dance by putting the tactics discussed in this chapter into practice. This will guarantee quick delivery, satisfied clients, and a successful online company. Always remember that efficiency is a constant state of improvement, therefore, to maintain long-term success on TikTok, keep an eye on, hone, and optimize your workflow.

Promoting Customer Loyalty: Establishing Credibility in the Changing TikTok E-Commerce Landscape

Long-term success in the rapidly changing world of TikTok e-commerce, where fads are king, depends on developing a loyal client base and earning their confidence. This subchapter explores the tactics and procedures that foster satisfying customer encounters and convert infrequent consumers into devoted brand ambassadors.

The Transparency and Authenticity Foundation of Trust

Authenticity and openness are the foundations of trust is how you build a strong foundation:

Correct Product Listings: Provide precise and thorough product descriptions along with excellent images. Clearly state the characteristics, attributes, and any possible restrictions of the product.

Achievable Shipping Approximations: Have reasonable shipping expectations. Indicate projected delivery dates in an understandable and open manner. When feasible, underpromise and overdeliver.Acknowledge and value User-Generated Content (UGC): Use UGC to showcase actual consumer experiences. Display client testimonials and images using your products to increase credibility and social proof.

Act Like a Human: Show off your brand's human side without fear. On TikTok, reply to messages and comments with a personal touch. Talk to your audience and establish a rapport with them.

The Foundations of Client Satisfaction: Keeping Your Words

Building happiness with customers requires meeting their expectations. Here's how to fulfill your commitments:

Effective Order Processing: Make an effort to process orders quickly and deliver them on schedule. To guarantee a seamless fulfillment process, put the techniques discussed in the preceding chapter—"Processing Orders Efficiently"—into practice.

Unambiguous Communication Throughout the Process: Ensure that your clients are informed at every stage of the procedure. Clearly marked purchase confirmations, shipment status updates, and quick response times for questions are all provided.

Resolving Concerns Quickly and Courteously: Errors occur, so It's important to handle any problems politely and quickly. As required, provide solutions, exchanges, or refunds to show that you are dedicated to making your customers happy.

Achieve Above and Beyond Whenever Possible: Make the additional effort to satisfy and surprise your clients. Give your customers special discounts, a handwritten thank-you message, or a tiny complimentary sample along with their purchase.

The Strength of Customer Service: Establishing Connections

Loyalty and trust are fostered by exceptional customer service. Here's how to succeed in this field:
Many Communication Channels: Offer a variety of channels for communicating with customers, including live chat, email, social network messaging, and even a phone hotline.
Sensitivity and Reactive Assistance: Teach your customer support staff to respond to requests from customers with empathy. Pay attention to what they have to say and strive to find practical answers.
Proactive Problem Solving: Foresee possible problems and take proactive measures to resolve them. Provide customer support information that is readily accessible, FAQs, and explicit return and refund procedures.
Important Client Input: Ask your consumers for comments on a regular basis. Use social media interactions, reviews, and polls to learn about their

requirements and make ongoing improvements to your products and services.

The Loyalty Loop: Cultivating Durable Connections

Programs for rewarding loyal customers might help you build stronger relationships with them. Think about these tactics:
Loyalty Programs: Put in place a loyalty program that gives early access to new items, discounts, points, or special incentives to loyal consumers.
Personalized Communication: Make sure all of your correspondence with clients is unique. Send personalized birthday wishes, incentives, and suggestions by using client data.
Building Communities: Develop a sense of community in relation to your brand. To foster a feeling of community, host engaging live broadcasts on TikTok, hold prizes or competitions, and promote consumer engagement.

The Tango of Trust

Gaining the trust and loyalty of your clients requires a constant dance between understanding them, exceeding their expectations, and meeting their needs. You can turn your TikTok e-commerce firm into a sanctuary of trust, happiness, and enduring client loyalty by embracing openness, placing a high priority on effective delivery, and providing exceptional customer service. Never forget that your clients are the lifeblood of your company. Make an investment in cultivating a solid rapport with them, and observe your company thrive on the dynamic platform of TikTok e-commerce.

Getting Through the Maze: Managing Client Questions and Complaints for Successful TikTok E-Commerce

A favorable company image and client loyalty are greatly enhanced by promptly answering concerns and complaints in the fast-paced world of TikTok e-commerce, where consumer interactions may happen as rapidly as viral trends. With the information and techniques in this chapter, you will be able to successfully negotiate this customer service labyrinth and turn any negative encounters into good ones that strengthen your bonds with your clients.

Knowing the Scene: Frequently Asked Questions and Issues by Customers

Half the fight is won when one is ready. Below is a summary of some typical questions and grievances from customers that you may run into:

Questions about Products: Consumers could have inquiries about the functionality, compatibility, size, or materials of the product. Be ready to respond with clarity and in-depth knowledge.

Questions About Order Status: Clients may wish to inquire about the progress of their order, including the processing stage, estimated delivery date, and confirmation of receipt. Offer an easy-to-use order tracking system or a clear communication channel.

Delivery Questions: Clients may have inquiries regarding shipping costs, projected delivery schedules, or available shipping choices. Provide precise shipping details and take proactive measures to resolve any possible issues.

Refund and Return Questions: Customers might want more information about your refund and return policies. Make sure the procedure for returns, exchanges, and damage claims is outlined in your policy, and that it is easily accessible.

Product Problems and Grievances: Customers may occasionally receive products that are damaged or have functional problems. Provide a defined procedure for addressing these circumstances and provide refunds, repairs, or replacements as necessary.

The Fundamentals of Effective Resolution: The Art of Active Listening

The cornerstone of effective customer service interactions is active listening. The following are some crucial tactics:

Pay Close Attention to Them: When interacting with a customer, give them your undivided attention. Avoid multitasking and focus on understanding their concerns fully.

Acknowledge Their Frustration: Validate their emotions. Acknowledge their frustration or disappointment and empathize with their situation.

Paraphrase and Confirm: Paraphrase their concerns to ensure understanding, and confirm you have grasped the issue accurately.

Ask Clarifying Questions: Don't be afraid to ask clarifying questions to gather all the necessary information before proposing a solution.

Crafting Effective Solutions: Resolving Inquiries and Addressing Complaints

The goal is to resolve inquiries and address complaints efficiently and satisfactorily. Here's how to achieve this:

Knowledge is Power: Equip your customer service team with in-depth product knowledge and a thorough understanding of your return and refund policies.

Offer Options: Whenever possible, offer a range of solutions to address the customer's concerns. This empowers them to choose the option that best suits their needs.

Transparency and Communication: Keep the customer informed throughout the resolution process. Communicate any delays, changes, or decisions clearly and immediately.

Go the Extra Mile: Sometimes, a little extra effort goes a long way. Consider providing a discount on a future purchase or a complementary product as a sign of goodwill.

Utilizing the Right Tools for the Job

Technology may speed communication and accelerate outcomes. Consider these tools:

Live Chat Functionality: Offer real-time chat support to answer quick inquiries and address concerns promptly.

Ticketing System: Implement a ticketing system to track customer inquiries and complaints, ensuring no issue falls through the cracks.

Knowledge Base: Develop a comprehensive knowledge base with FAQs, product information, and troubleshooting guides to empower customers to find answers independently.

The Power of Positivity: Turning Negatives into Positives

Even negative interactions can be turned into positive experiences. Here's how to approach challenging situations:

Maintain a Professional Demeanor: Remain calm, professional, and courteous even in the face of frustration or anger.

Apologize for Inconveniences: Acknowledge any mistakes or shortcomings and sincerely apologize for any inconvenience caused.

** Pay Attention to Solutions:** Turn your attention from the issue to the potential fix. Describe the actions you plan to take to make things right.

Request Input: Once the problem has been resolved, get client input regarding your service. Make use of this knowledge to keep refining your customer service strategy.

Conclusion: The Customer Service Symphony

Handling customer inquiries and complaints effectively requires a well-orchestrated symphony of active listening, clear communication, and a focus on solutions. By equipping your team with the right knowledge, tools, and a positive attitude, you can transform these interactions into opportunities to strengthen customer relationships and build brand loyalty. Remember, a satisfied customer is a loyal customer, and loyalty is the key to long-term success in the ever-evolving world of TikTok e-commerce. So, conduct your customer service symphony with care, and watch your brand resonate positively with your audience.

Chapter Five

A Peep into the Crystal Ball: New Developments Influencing TikTok E-Commerce's Future

The TikTok e-commerce industry is a dynamic, ever-changing, and very promising field. This chapter explores new trends that will likely influence how people purchase on the platform in the future, giving you the tools you need to remain ahead of the curve and take advantage of these exciting changes.

Live Streaming's Ascent: An Epic Social Shopping Event
On TikTok, live stream purchasing is quickly taking off, turning the site into a bustling bazaar full of people interacting in real time. This is what to anticipate:
Interactive Product Demonstrations: Companies will use live streaming to show off their items, respond to queries from viewers instantly, and make shopping more dynamic and interesting.

Influencer Marketing on Steroids: There will be an even greater frequency of live streaming with well-known TikTok influencers. To increase sales, these dependable individuals will launch new goods, provide special deals, and instill a feeling of urgency.

Entertainment and Gamification: To keep viewers interested and encourage purchases, gamification features like freebies, competitions, and interactive polls will be included in live broadcasts.

The Influence of Local Business: Creating Loyalty via Common Experiences

Building a community will be essential to TikTok e-commerce's success in the future. How can companies take advantage of this trend?

Brand Hashtags and Challenges: Utilize branded hashtags and challenges to promote user-generated content. Customers may become brand ambassadors, and a sense of community is fostered as a result.

Social Proof and User Reviews: Highlight gratifying client testimonials and user-generated material with happy clients using your items. Social proof encourages people to join society and fosters trust.

Rewarding Consistent Clientele: Establish loyalty programs that provide early access to new items, exclusive community events, or exclusive discounts to loyal consumers.

The Blending of Realities: AR and VR Become Main Players Technologies like virtual reality (VR) and augmented reality (AR) have the potential to completely change the TikTok e-commerce experience. Here's a look at what lies ahead:

Virtual Try-On Experiences: AR filters will enable buyers to virtually try on accessories, cosmetics, or clothing before making a purchase, resulting in better judgments and a lower percentage of returns.

360° Product Tours: Virtual reality (VR) will allow consumers to visually examine things in a 360° setting, making shopping more realistic and engaging.

The Fusion of Realities: AR and VR Ascent to the Front **

Customers will feel more confident in their purchasing selections when they can see furniture or décor in their own homes before making a purchase, thanks to augmented reality technology.

The Rise of Conversational Commerce: Voice Assistants and Chatbots Simplify Purchasing One major factor in making the buying experience simpler will be conversational commerce.

How to do it is as follows:

Chatbots driven by AI: Artificial intelligence (AI)-driven chatbots may respond to user inquiries, suggest products, and even carry out transactions using the TikTok chat interface.

Voice Commerce Integration: TikTok will be connected with voice assistants such as Google Assistant and Amazon Alexa. This will enable users to search for goods, add things to baskets, and even finish transactions using voice commands.

Smooth Integration of Shopping: There will be more blurring of the distinctions between researching, browsing, and buying. Anticipate a smooth transition where consumers can find goods, interact with them to learn more about them, and easily finish transactions.

The Fusion of Realities: AR and VR Ascent to the Front

There are a ton of intriguing opportunities for TikTok e-commerce in the future. Businesses are able to create dynamic and engaging shopping experiences that increase sales and encourage brand loyalty by keeping up with evolving trends and adopting cutting-edge technology. As always, the secret to success is to be flexible, creative, and always looking for new methods to engage your audience on this dynamic platform. Thus, keep an eye out for change, look forward, and see how your TikTok e-commerce company takes off.

Keeping Up with the Times: Competitive Approaches for TikTok E-Commerce's Future

The bustling marketplace of TikTok e-commerce is a dynamic environment. Achieving success and carving out a niche requires staying one step ahead of the competition. This chapter provides you with innovative tactics to help you stay ahead of the competition in the constantly changing world of TikTok business.

Understanding the Competitive Environment

Gaining an advantage starts with having a deep awareness of your competitors' markets. Here's how to get a sharp image:
Identify Your Key Rivals: Look up and categorize your TikTok competitors, both direct and indirect. Examine their product offers, price structures, customer involvement strategies, and content strategies.
Analyze their TikTok profiles, engagement rates, follower demographics, and most popular content forms to get further into analysis. Determine their advantages and disadvantages to guide your own approach.
Benchmarking Performance: Monitor your own performance indicators, such as conversion rates, engagement levels, and follower growth. Compare these stats with those of your rivals to find areas that need work.

Writing Strategic and Engaging Content: Content Is King (and Queen)
The secret to success in the quick-paced world of TikTok is creating engaging material. The following

are some tips for creating strategic content that beats the competition:

Trendjacking with a Twist: Take advantage of popular hashtags and challenges, but add your own distinctive value proposition and brand identity. Instead of copying others, produce original, captivating content that gains traction.

Resonant Storytelling: Narratives evoke a response in people. Create stories that show off your items in use, emphasize the advantages they provide, and stir up emotions in the audience.

Accept User-Generated Content (UGC): Motivate clients to provide media that highlights your offerings. UGC promotes genuineness, increases trust, and highlights the practical benefits that your products provide.

Try Different Formats: Don't be scared to try different content formats, such as quick product demonstrations, behind-the-scenes looks, influencer partnerships, or instructional guides.

Customization is Vitality: Adapting Your Strategy to Various Audiences

A one-size-fits-all strategy is insufficient. For optimum effect, customize your content approach as follows:

Audience Segmentation: Divide up your intended audience into groups according to their purchasing habits, interests, and demographics. This enables you to modify your message and content so that it appeals to certain client groups.

Take Advantage of TikTok's Targeting Options: Make use of the comprehensive targeting features offered by TikTok to direct your content towards the people who are most likely to be interested in your offerings.

Micro-Influencer Marketing: Collaborate with pertinent micro-influencers who closely relate to a certain niche market. Compared to widespread celebrity endorsements, this focused strategy may result in better engagement and conversion rates.

Successful Optimization: Data-Driven Choices for Ongoing Improvement: Never work in the dark.

Here's how to use data to improve your approach:*
Monitor Key Performance Indicators (KPIs): Pay particular attention to important metrics like as conversion rates, click-through rates, impressions, and engagement rates.

Examine Performance Data: Dig further by determining which influencer relationships, hashtags, and content types provide the greatest outcomes.

A/B Testing is Your Friend: See which iterations of your content, ad text, and CTAs (calls to action) work best with your audience by continuously testing them.

Embrace Experimentation: Don't be scared to try out novel concepts and modify your strategy in response to data and audience input.

The Innovation Need: Using Cutting-Edge Technologies

TikTok e-commerce has a bright future full of technical innovations. Here's how to keep on top of things:

Integration of Augmented Reality (AR): Make use of AR filters to enable buyers to virtually try on merchandise or see how it might seem in their own setting.

Conversational Commerce: Investigate how artificial intelligence (AI)-powered chatbots may be used to provide product suggestions, respond to consumer inquiries, and expedite the purchasing process.

Live Stream Shopping Extravaganza: To increase sales and audience engagement, host captivating live streams with influencer partnerships, product demos, and interactive features like freebies and competitions.

Creating a Faithful Community: Encouraging Prolonged Client Connect
Success is more than just a single transaction. Here's how to create a devoted following for your brand:*
Respond to Comments and Messages: In order to actively interact with your audience, make sure you swiftly and politely address any comments and messages you get.
Reward Loyalty: Put in place loyalty schemes that reward recurring purchases and create a sense of community.

Scaling the Heights: Methods for Growing Your E-Commerce Empire on TikTok
The e-commerce space on TikTok has enormous development potential. This chapter gives you the cutting-edge tactics you need to grow your company, beyond its present constraints and achieve unprecedented success on a dynamic platform.
Establishing a Long-Term Basis: Enhancing Your Main Functions Make sure all of your core activities are functioning properly before expanding.

You should concentrate here:* **Effective Order Fulfillment:** Follow the guidelines for effective order fulfillment provided in the preceding chapter (Processing Orders Efficiently). Give prompt delivery and open communication with clients top priority.

Excellent Customer Service: Create a customer service plan centered on pleasant interactions, timely communication, and effective handling of questions and complaints (see Handling Customer Inquiries and Complaints).

Using data to inform decisions, track key performance indicators (KPIs) to pinpoint areas in need of improvement. Make the most of data insights to improve your overall approach, advertising efforts, and content strategy.

Extending Your Influence: Successful Audience Acquisition Techniques Gaining new clients is essential to expansion.

Here are a few successful tactics:

 Organic material growth: Produce interesting, well-written material that appeals to your target market. To develop a solid organic following, take part in challenges, use storytelling, and make use of popular hashtags.

Paid Advertising: Use TikTok's advertising tools to target certain interests, behaviors, and demographics. To grab attention and encourage conversions, use powerful ad layouts and eye-catching images.

Influencer Marketing: Assemble a team of relevant TikTok influencers that share the same values as your target market and brand identity. When it comes to engagement rates, micro-influencers often outperform famous endorsements.

Collaborations and Cross-Promotion: To reach new audiences, work with creators to reach them or partner with complimentary companies for cross-promotional efforts.

Diversification of Content: Investigating Novel Formats and Approaches

Avoid getting into a rut. Here's how to vary your approach to article creation:

Try Various Formats: Go beyond brief product presentations and investigate longer guides, behind-the-scenes looks, instructional materials, or humorous skits that creatively present your items.

Live Stream Shopping Extravaganza: In order to increase sales and audience engagement, host engaging live streams with influencer partnerships, product demos, special deals, Q&A sessions, and gamified components like giveaways and competitions.

Power of User-Generated Content (UGC): Promote user-generated content by holding competitions or challenges that reward clients for producing material that highlights your goods. UGC promotes genuineness, increases trust, and highlights the practical benefits that your products provide.

Scalability Optimization: Making Use of Technology and Automation

Technology has the capacity to accelerate growth and simplify processes. Here's how to make the most of it:

Social Media Management Tools: Plan your content, monitor performance indicators across platforms, and effectively manage your online presence with the help of social media management tools.

Inventory Management Software: Make sure you have the items in stock to satisfy rising demand by using reliable inventory management software to monitor stock levels and streamline fulfillment procedures.

Analytics and Reporting Tools: Make use of these resources to learn more about the demographics of your audience, the efficacy of your material, and the campaign. Make use of these insights to hone your approach and maximize development.

Creating a Successful Team: Growing Your Staff

As your company grows, think about assembling a committed staff. The following are some important roles:

Content Creators: Invest in skilled content producers who are familiar with the TikTok platform and can provide interesting material that appeals to your intended audience.

Customer Service Representatives: Grow your customer service department to guarantee that complaints and inquiries from customers are handled promptly and competently.

Data Analysts

Employ data analysts to analyze performance indicators, spot patterns, and provide insightful analysis to guide strategic choices.

The World Market Is Here: Examining International Growth

You have the whole world at your disposal. Here are some ways to look into growing internationally:

Localization is Key: Modify your product offerings, marketing strategy, and content strategy to appeal to global consumers. Take into account regional trends, cultural quirks, and linguistic challenges.

Regulation Compliance: Before reaching out to new nations, make sure that you are in compliance with shipping standards and international commerce laws.

Partnering with Local Influencers: Assist local influencers who are familiar with the local context and have the ability to successfully engage your target audience in certain areas.

The Symphony in Scale

Effectively growing your TikTok e-commerce company requires a well crafted blend of tactics. To perform your growth song, you'll need to optimize your core processes, enlarge your audience, diversify your material, use technology, and assemble a committed staff. Keep in mind that TikTok e-commerce has a bright future ahead of it.

The Changing Encore: Important Lessons and Concluding Remarks on the Prospects for TikTok E-Commerce

The TikTok e-commerce industry is a vibrant, ever-evolving platform that is full of opportunities. Here is a powerful recap of the main lessons learned and parting reflections to help you on your path as we draw to a conclusion on this exploration:

Data's Power
The key to success in TikTok e-commerce is data. Maintaining close tabs on important metrics like impressions, engagement rates, and conversion rates gives you essential information about what appeals to your audience and what needs work. Utilize this information to assess the success of your efforts, improve your targeting strategy, and optimize your content plan. Accept A/B testing and never stop experimenting to find the best combinations that will grow your company.

Establishing Community and Trust
Long-term success in the transient world of social media is based on community and trust. Be truthful

when describing your products, conservative when estimating delivery times, and receptive when interacting with customers. Encourage user-generated content, hold interactive live streaming, and give loyal consumers rewards to build a sense of community. Prioritizing the development of a community and trust lays the groundwork for long-lasting client connections and steady growth.

The Content Dilemma The king (or queen) of TikTok e-commerce is compelling content. Go beyond basic product presentations and create compelling stories that highlight the benefits of your goods. Try experimenting with various forms, such as quick product demonstrations, instructive tutorials, or memorable sketches that draw viewers in. Accept the power of narrative, take advantage of popular hashtags, and don't be scared to include a little bit of your brand's own personality in your content mix. Recall that sincerity makes an impression.

The Revolution in Technology: TikTok e-commerce is heavily reliant on technical improvements for the future. Customers will be able to digitally try on things or see them in their own locations thanks to augmented reality (AR). AI chatbots enabling conversational commerce will expedite communication and provide prompt customer service. Extravaganzas of live streaming shopping will turn shopping into a communal and participatory event. In order to remain ahead of the curve and provide your consumers with a flawless shopping experience, embrace this cutting-edge technology.

Take Charge of Your Future, Mold Your Course
TikTok e-commerce has an unwritten future full of opportunities just waiting to be discovered. You can control your own fate on this fascinating platform by keeping up with new trends, modifying your approach to fit the changing environment, and always looking for fresh approaches to engage your audience. Thus, make the most of data, foster a sense of community and trust, provide engaging content, and welcome technological innovation. You can turn your TikTok e-commerce presence into a booming success story by following these guiding ideas. Never forget that the future is yours to seize; leave your imprint on the rapidly changing TikTok e-commerce landscape.

www.ingramcontent.com/pod-product-compliance
Lightning Source LLC
Chambersburg PA
CBHW070203230526
45471CB00002B/794